2

Lessons
in Love My Maw Taught Me
and Other Memorable Stories

Deborah Gray

Copyright © 2018 Deborah Gray.

All rights reserved, no part of this book may be used to reproduced by any means, graphic, electronic, or mechanical, including photocopying, recording, taping or by any information storage retrieval system without the written permission of the author except in the case of brief quotations embodied in critical articles and reviews.

Edited by Ryan Sergent – Payne, Independent Editor

Editor Contact Information

Email: ryan_sergent@live.com

Library of Congress Control Number: 2018903349

ISBN: 978-0-692-09227-9

Contents

One -Rose Wilson • 7

Two - Decoration Day • 10

Three - The Pink Commode • 13

Four - School • 15

Five - The Perm • 21

Six - Church • 23

Seven - The Washing Machine • 28

Eight - The Hiding • 30

Nine - Bible Camp • 33

Ten - The Princess Dress • 37

Eleven – Tobacco • 40

Twelve - Turtle Soup • 45

Thirteen - Golden's Creek • 49

Fourteen - Cinnamon Rolls • 53

Fifteen - Labor Day • 55

Sixteen - The Lady Schick • 58

Seventeen - The Wake • 61

Eighteen - Hugh Charles • 64
Nineteen - Breakfast • 69
Twenty - Voting Day • 75
Twenty-One - The Sweepstakes • 78
Twenty-Two - Military Funeral • 81
Twenty-Three - Aunt Vina • 84
Twenty-Four - The Swimming Pool • 87
Twenty-Five - The Car Wreck • 90
Twenty-Six - Tom T. Hall • 93
Twenty-Seven - Learning To Crochet • 96
Twenty-Eight - The Uniform • 99
Twenty-Nine - Traveler's Inn • 102
Thirty - Laughter • 105
Thirty-One - My Babies • 111
Thirty-Two - Girlfriends • 116
Thirty-Three - Scotch • 120
Thirty-Four - Bus Monitor • 123
Thirty-Five - The Day My World Stopped • 129

Chapter 1
Rose Wilson

Rose Wilson was an enigma. Born Rosa Etta Reynolds on January 6th, 1903 to Wesley Reynolds and Josephine Peace Reynolds beside the Cumberland River in Whitley County Kentucky (what was once considered the Underground Railroad to Canada during the middle of the 1800's). She had three sisters and one brother. If I could say anything about my lineage it would be that all the women were strong, independent, and self-confident. I never knew my great grandmother, but was told she could shoot a walnut off a tree at fifty feet and she was a dead shot. I knew my grandmother and I would tend to agree. My Maw could handle any kind of firearm and expected her offspring to be able to do the same. She could do or be anything, but to me she was just Maw. She was fifty-three years old when I was born and had lived a lifetime. She married Jim Wilson in 1920, birthed six children, raised five to adulthood and had eleven grandchildren, me being number four.

    I was her shadow for the early part of my life. These stories are my memories of that time. They are colored by the emotions and realities of a small child and the times when they existed. In writing my little stories I had no idea the impact Maw had had on my life until I stopped to reread them. From every aspect she influenced me and who I was to become. At the time I was just enjoying her presence and the wisdom she imparted. She, like all the women of her family, was independent to a fault and had tempers bordering on dangerous. She could shoot a deer or rabbit and skin it. She could butcher a hog and render the fat. She could walk ten miles to deliver a baby! She knew the herbs and wild plants of the mountains. She could dig ginseng or yellow root with the best of them. And on any given Sunday she could raise the roof singing "Shall We Gather at the River" at Locust Grove Baptist Church. She didn't wear pants until 1975 when Brent, my son, was born. She wore them under her dresses for years, then one day she just up and took to wearing them like everyone else.

    She loved her family. Those alive and those dead. She tended the graves of her loved ones with the care of a loving nurse. She gardened with abandoned fervor. She loved to see things grow, plants and children alike. Her passion was for life, all forms of it and when something or someone died, a little piece of her went with it! I learned the true meaning of grief as it was etched on her face, when she lost her baby boy. All the things I learned about life and the love of it I owe to my Maw. But most of all, I learned to laugh. And I hope you do too, as you read my little stories, mostly inspired by her and dedicated to her. Because had it not been for her, I would not be here to tell them.

Chapter 2
Decoration Day

Decoration Day in 1958 my cousin Karen was twenty – eight months old. Older than me. She was blonde and blue eyed and had a head full of curly hair. I on the other hand had none or very little. My Aunt Zona, my mother's brother Raleigh's wife, would make our dresses to wear to Decoration Day! Mine would be blue and Karen's would be pink. They would have crinoline slips underneath that would be starched stiff! Mom and Zona decided they would buy new socks and frilly special panties to go with our dresses. This was a treat! In 1958 my Daddy was going to school at Cumberland College on the G.I. Bill and money was tight, real tight. And Uncle Raleigh only worked sporadically! So, spending the few extra dollars was a luxury.

    The cemeteries back then had no grass. None! Each little family plot had little wood picket fences around it. Some had wired ones. They were swept clean to remove any sign of grass or weed. Women, the week before would make tissue paper flowers to adorn the graves. Some would dip them in candle wax. My Maw was very adept at that! On this day my mother was very excited to greet her cousins and that was when she let me get away from her. My cousin Karen always stood very still. Like a store doll, my mother used to say. Not a hair out of place with her pink ruffled dress and lace panties on. Me on the other hand was nowhere to be found! Of course, Maw found me! Sitting on a newly dug grave, were red clay mud filling my ruffled panties full! They said you could hear my Mother scream to the head of Golden's Creek! I was covered from the waist down in red clay mud. No one got to see my ruffled panties.

    I saw a post recently about a Decoration Day this month at Ketcham Cemetery. In the South, Decoration Day is a big occasion! It was started in the South after the civil war to commemorate their dead soldiers after the Yankees mistreated their bodies. Good widow women had them decentered and reburied in reputable family plots in the South. It is noted that thousands of our southern men were removed from Gettysburg and sent South. Memorial Day was devised by the Union but the southern states, not recognizing it, had their own. My family's is the first Sunday after the first Monday in June. Well how about that!

It is a reunion of sorts and back in the day all the family that went up North to work after the second World War, you know Detroit, Chicago, Crestline Ohio, etc., came home. We all got new hats, shoes and dresses! We put the" big pot in the little one " my Maw used to say. In other words, we killed the fatted calf! In 1958 I was not quite two years old and the bane of my mothers' existence! I had already kicked out her front teeth while she was diapering me and yet, I was the apple of her eye!? My mother was twenty - six when I was born. Late for a southern woman! She had been married a long time, eight years, and she had suffered numerous miscarriages before my arrival. This would be the first Decoration Day when my far-off relatives would meet me!

Chapter 3
The Pink Commode

This morning I saw a pink commode sitting beside the road and it made me think of my Mother. Not because it was pink, but because of something that happened fifty-six years ago! We were a military family. My earliest recollections are of Navy bases and housings. We traveled like nomads wherever Daddy was sent. One such place was Newport, Rhode Island. I wasn't much out of diapers and potty training was a grand endeavor at three and a half.

My dad's cousin, Floretta and her husband, were also stationed with us. Mom and Floretta loved to shop! They liked the PX but Sears was better. Her and Mom were like Lucy and Ethel, young women fresh out of the hills of Kentucky. They were always getting into trouble. I loved them!

  While in Sears shopping Mom and Floretta lost me! In those days it was similar to Lowes. You could buy anything there from clothes to high end appliances. When I was found I was sitting on a pink commode with a stream of yellow water running down the aisle! I was told, she scooped me up, like the devil himself was after her, hoping that was all I had done!

After that, there were numerous episodes of me getting into trouble, but I never peed in Sears again!

Chapter 4
School

I loved school! From the very first day I could not wait until the big yellow bus pulled up to get me! The night before, I was so excited I hardly slept. I was six years old! Not four or five or even three, as they do now but 6. They made me wait until I was six, but I would make up for it. I had the paper and the pencils and MY BOOKS! YES, MY BOOKS! For years my Father had been sending me a book a month thru the Book of the Month Club. And I could read and I wanted to share. Share the Brothers Grimm and Black Beauty, but mostly my favorite The Little Mermaid. I had my book bag and my penny loafers on and I was ready.

Upon arriving at school, I encountered those not so enamored with the idea of higher learning. Cries could be heard from one end of the hall to the other. I couldn't understand! I was mesmerized by all the new smells; chalk, pine tar and fresh lavender from the teacher! After a while things began to settle down and the cries dulled to batted breathes of sobs and tears gently rolling down cheeks as they resigned themselves that they would have to stay this day, but tomorrow was another day. I got my alphabetically assigned seat. I would sit behind Sam Carr for eight years! But this day I was so happy to just to be there! The teacher began by asking each of us did we have anything we wanted to share with our new classmates! Oh. my hand went up quick, flailing about every which way! She of course picked me. I pulled out my book on The Little Mermaid. I was so excited! I began to explain it and not read it. I felt I could give it a more in-depth review than just Hans Christian Anderson's version. Also, it had pictures and there was nothing like a little show and tell!

Let me explain! My version of the book had beautiful art work. It had pictures that hung in the Louvre and other European art houses. The mermaids depicted were nude from the waste up! My teacher apparently did not check my reading material before my Show – and – tell. Every six-year-old boy in my class was beyond fascinated as I proceeded to review my book! That was until Sharon Mayne stood up and said, "MISS FAULKNER, SHE HAS NO CLOTHES ON!" Miss Faulkner stepped around, looked at my book and proceeded to shut down my highly enthusiastic review! I was upset that my presentation had been cut short but would be even more so when she confiscated my book! She kept it all day long! My precious gift from my Father! At the end of the day it was returned with the preamble to not bring it back, and when I opened it to my beautiful pictures the offensive parts had been blacked out with markers!!! Oh!!! Even at six years old I was appalled! My beautiful book so defaced!! I cried all the way home. My first day of school so ruined for me. My mother seeing my tears and hearing my story became enraged and made a trip to see Miss Faulkner!

I never knew what was said but I did know my Mother. I never took one of my beautiful books to school again, but she never stopped me from reading them.

***

This afternoon I noticed Knox County has moved up in the world. We have accrued Graffiti artists!! But I am here to tell you they weren't' the first, I was!

I loved school. When I started school, we didn't have kindergarten. They threw you in the deep end, sink or swim. Get ready First grade! I was lucky! I had been reading FOREVER! Or for as long as I could remember. Remember I was grown at six!

My Daddy had ordered me the Book of the Month Club. I got Black Beauty, Grimm's Fairy Tales, The Little Mermaid (which they banned when I brought it to school, another story) and all the other classics from the time I could walk. I learned first to read by sight, then when I ran up on a word I didn't know I sounded it out. Later I learned it was phonics. So, when I started school and I was handed the Dick and Jane book I made quick work out of it! After maybe fifteen minutes I handed it back and asked for another. I was eager to see if Spot learned any new tricks!

Not only was school fascinating I got a whole new wardrobe. Mom ordered me five new dresses from the Sears Roebuck catalog. I still remember them. One was a pink pin stripe seersucker just like cousin Floretta's. It had spaghetti straps and smocking across the bosom! There was a green and orange Irish plaid and a blue gingham and a brown check with little orange flowers on it. I didn't much care for it. And my next favorite was the red corduroy with the white blouse trimmed in red! Daddy had gone to Bailey's country store and bought me new penny loafers and in each were bright new pennies.

Next, I discovered there were little boys in my class. One especially caught my eye. I thought he looked just like a young Ricky Nelson! He wore brylcreem in his hair and it laid in waves! Oh My Gosh! He wore new black converse tennis shoes and wrangler jeans rolled up. He had on a white tee shirt and a blue plaid shirt and to top it off for a six-year-old boy, he had all his teeth! sharp! I was in love. How could I make my love known? At recess I spied what could be my canvas as I watched him cross the playground to the freshly white washed concrete block outhouse. AH HAH! This would be my masterpiece! He would have to fall in love with me now! So, at the most opportune moment I procured my crayons, the big fat ones made for little children. These would work so fine: A green, a red, a yellow and a blue. My creative juices were flowing, even then! At lunch I had a plan. I would write in multi colors: I LOVE TERRY SAILOR. I spelled Saylor wrong as I didn't know the correct spelling!

I accomplished my feat, and was very proud of my penmanship until I had been seen by none other than my own Great Aunt Velma

Baldwin, a fifth-grade teacher, looking out the window of her classroom. Well needless to say my excellent foray into the art world had consequences that left little to the imagination. One punishment incurred was to wash down that side of the boy's outhouse! To this day I can remember the odor of that outhouse, and I don't think Terry Saylor ever fell in love with me!

Chapter 5
The Perm

Last night I dyed my hair, and needless to say, it didn't go well! I have been accused on numerous occasions of being a hair abuser! Well, I concur, but to my defense I can't take all the blame. It began at an early age and was started by none other than my Mother! Vanity notwithstanding, I was born with and to this day have very little hair. Not only that it is mousey brown, the color of lint from a vacuum cleaner.

My cousins all had beautiful hair. Long and luxurious. Some dark, like my mother, some blonde and curly, and some dark red auburn, like my cousin Henrietta's; whose hair I envied and to this day dye mine to emulate.

My mother decided I must have a perm. Back then home perms were the rage and they even made them for "little" girls. The "Tonette!"

In January 1960 my Mother was eight

months pregnant with Tami, and she decided to give me a "Tonette"! Now remember I am four years old! My mother like Maw believed if a little was good, more was better! So, she used the most rollers she could and tightened them ever so tight. But the crux of the matter set in when she applied the setting lotion!

I have always been sensitive to odors of any kind but this stuff stunk! The more she put on, the more I wiggled. The more she threatened, the more I squirmed. Finally, I got free and I ran. I ran under the bed and hid. I knew she couldn't get me there! She was too fat! She bent down and yelled and yelled! I can still see her now, reaching and reaching with me deflecting her arms from side to side.

Finally, she got a broomstick thinking she could flush me out but I was just like a rabbit! It went on until Mom's brother HC came and crawled in after me. The jig was up! Another whipping, but this time a new hairdo to boot! From the pictures dated February '60 Maw and Paw's birthday dinner I had the first Afro of the '60's!

Chapter 6
Church

This Sunday morning, I am remembering many others, mostly my Maw. The weekends spent with her definitely would have Sunday School and Church as her top priority!

When she lived "up on the hill" in Golden's Creek we walked the mile or so to church. My cousins Barb Gatliff, Eunice Mays and Lucille Terry lived up there too. There were many others, but we had a little group that sat together at church. I so looked forward to walking to church on that dirt road! Maw had a few, how should I say it, quirks! Mommy had bought me this cute little sun dress just like my cousin Floretta's, pink pin stripe seer sucker with spaghetti straps. I loved that dress, I wore it forever! The bodice was elastic and mommy kept letting out the hem.

The problem was it had no sleeves. I thought it was just perfect and in July and August you didn't want to wear a sweater, but Maw wouldn't have it! I would cover my arms in the house of the Lord. Well Maw let me walk to Sunday School with my friends and she and Paw would come later in his old '56 black Chevy truck. So, me, being me, decided she would never know, I chucked my little yellow sweater behind the seat at church! I would retrieve it later!

I loved Sunday School. All the stories! The felt mats with the colorful cut outs of biblical characters depicting dramatic stories. Later on, I would experience one myself! Getting into church I forgot all about my sweater! Shortly before church was to start I looked up seeing my grandparents coming up the steps. As I went to retrieve my sweater it was nowhere to be found! My older cousin Jimmy Mays had thought it would be funny to hide it! It was funny alright. It was to be my death. I was sure of it. My Maw looked at me and I at her, and it was the evil eye. For those of you who do not know, it is worse than death at Brushy Mountain to a 6-year-old!

For the whole church service, I could think of nothing but what awaited when it was over. So, I devised a plan to leave church early and beat Maw home! Bad, bad idea. A whipping for taking off and losing my sweater was one thing, but skipping church was another. Needless to say, when Mom came to get me not only did I suffer one whipping, but I got two! Until this day I cannot go in a church without my arms covered!

***

Growing up in a southern church was the foundation of everything!! From the time you were born to the time you were planted in your families' cemetery it was your one true constant. My Maw and Paw had two homes. One "on the hill," their old home place and the other down by our church, Locust Grove. They had owned the house on the hill opposite of it, but now my Aunt Shirley, Uncle Clifford and my cousin Dennis lived there. Down the road apiece was where Aunt Ruth and her family lived. Another house my grandparents once owned! So not only was church the figurative center of our lives, it literally was!

    The summer of 1964 Aunt Shirley was pregnant with David, who came in November. This was August and Oh So Hot! Brother Roy Girdner was having a revival. How I remember I had a huge crush on his son Troy! IT WAS HOT! And all the church windows were open with all the good ladies fanning themselves with paper fans adorned by famous artworks of

Jesus or the Lord's Supper, provided by any one of the fine Funeral Homes! Church usually held late. Old time Baptists were like that! They followed the spirit and if it moved, you didn't! For a nine-year-old that was torture! My cousin Den was seven and a follower, but this night he had found some comrades and he began to bait me. It didn't take much. I was bored and hot. The first time he pulled my hair I glared at him from across the seat. Next, he eased up and pinched me! By now I was sworping at him and caught the eye of my Maw! She looked down and squinted, not too bad, yet!

    During the service there is an altar call, and after "the lowly misbegotten" had chosen to accept the Lord, all the kindly Christian men and women prayed at the altar! Being a good "Christian" I too bowed my head, for fear that Maw might raise hers and see me not praying! I had almost got the evil eye once that day! I was treading on thin ice! While my head was bowed and I was concentrating someone grabbed my ankles and I squalled like Jesus had touched my soul! Everyone raised up and looked. Maw spied me; THE EVIL EYE! Den had crawled under the pews and waited until just the right time to get me!

Aunt Shirley got Den and I can still see her with that willow switch burning his legs up going up the hill beside the church, her six months pregnant! My "tee" was yet to come and I knew it. Church was no place for "shenanigans" she would say as I got my reward! My Maw loved church and instilled in us a love for it! As I grew up I look back and crave one more night of church with her singing, "Peace in the Valley!"

MAW'S PEACH COBBLER
1 large 20 oz. can of sliced peaches
1 tbsp of fresh lemon juice
1/2 cup sugar more or less to taste
1/8 cup cinnamon sugar (brown sugar with cinnamon mixed)
2 cups bisquick
1/2 to 3/4 cup milk
1/4 cup butter or margarine
Heat your oven to 400 degrees...In a bowl mix all your dry ingredients, then mix milk until it becomes like a doughy mixture. In a 9x13 greased with butter pan add your peaches and lemon juice, then dollop your bisquick mixture over the top. Top with little pats of butter and sprinkle cinnamon sugar over the top. Bake for 35minutes or until golden brown. Mmmmm

Chapter 7

The Washing Machine

This morning I have been doing laundry and thinking back when I used to help Maw do hers!

I hate laundry! There was a time when it was an adventure though. Maw didn't have good water, so she caught rain water in big barrels from the tin roof of the house. It was clear and clean and soft. Sometimes I would take my hands and run thru it to feel the silkiness of it. She boiled it in a big cast iron kettle out back to put in the old wringer washer. It had a gasoline engine and it banged and spit and sputtered. It was a wonder. I was fascinated! I wanted to operate the wringers. I just knew I could do it better than anyone else. "You'll get your arm caught and they'll have to cut it off" she said! As if that would put the fear of God in me! I would not be deterred. I watched and watched and first chance I got, I leapt into action! This day I had on my regular uniform, a tee shirt under boy's overalls. My mother found out early on, "Pollyanna" dresses and Knickerbocker shorts could not withstand me. My uncle HC called me Blues, indicating my overalls.

Well I found my Paw's shirt. I thought I would try it first. It was going just fine until one of my loose suspenders caught in the shirt sleeve! Oh no, I thought. I was caught! Maw was nowhere in sight and the monster had caught me and was going to eat me alive!

I started screaming at the top of my lungs! Maw came running, and in what seemed like seconds I was out of my overalls sitting in the altogether crying; dirty tears running down my face! For a six-year-old that was as close to death as I had ever been, I remember Maw's smell as I buried my head in her bosoms. They were big and soft and smelled of cashmere bouquet bath powder! How I would love to do that again.

Chapter 8
The Hiding

I lost Rockie yesterday! I literally lost him! I searched and searched and yelled and cried and could not find the little booger anywhere! He was nowhere to be found.

I knew exactly then how my mother must have felt years ago when it happened to her. In 1962 my father got sick. He was thirty years old. On this day my parents were going to Louisville to the V.A. Hospital for tests and my sister and I were to be left in the competent care of Moms baby brother HC and newlywed wife Judy. I loved HC. He was twenty – four, and full of fun. He asked me once what I wanted for Christmas. Me, maybe four years old, said a screwdriver. He said what kind, I told him I thought probably a Phillips. I was on top of things even then!

His new wife, Judy was another story. She was beautiful; dark European looking. She favored Sophia Loren. Tall and from my point of view at six years old stupid! My sister Tami was a baby and got all the attention, so I decided I would divert it. My parents had built a small ranch home. It had four rooms; kitchen, dining, living and bedroom. The dining room held the baby bed and a rollaway bed. For those of you who do not know what a rollaway bed is, it is a small half bed that folds up and most of the time is covered to try to hide the fact it is a rollaway bed.

My genius plan was to hide. They would search, thus making me the center of attention! I waited until they were glued to Tami and I hid. I slithered between the metal bars and the rollers of the rollaway bed. I pulled the fringe from the cover down low, I can still see it in my mind. It was red Hollyhocks with red fringe. I never as much as breathed hard for fear they would see the movement. I can still remember how I held my breath while they were yelling and screaming and crying for me! My plan was working! How long I laid there before drifting off to sleep I will never know, but the next thing I knew my mother was waking me up! She was so happy to see me; I suppose that was why I did not get a whipping! She must have thought I hid and went to sleep not hearing HC and Judy because if she thought

I had heard them it would've been something like "Lock Deb in the Attic"!

Some months later I pulled a similar prank with a lot less finesse. I slipped off from Maw and went to Aunt Shirley's to play with Den. She found me and I didn't sit down for a week!

By the way, I found Rockie. He was under my Recliner the whole time. He got a spanking too!

Chapter 9
Bible Camp

This morning I was reminded by John Logan of a time and a place so dear to my childhood. In Whitley County where I grew up there was a man who visited the schools named Mr. Minturn (Mrs.Wahlsted in Knox). He was very tall and bald with a snow-white fringe circling from ear to ear. He wore horn rimmed glasses and had a big toothy grin. We looked forward to his visits. He would play an accordion, and we would sing Bible songs and then he would tell us a Bible story with the aid of a felt mat and colorful cut outs. It was wonderful! He even had rewards. Daily devotionals, old and new testaments, full bibles and eventually Bible Camp! Oh My! I was going for that! I had never been to camp, but I wanted to go! There were pamphlets indicating what would be offered: Hiking, baseball, all sorts of activities, and in small text Bible study, old and New Testament with church services nightly. No problem! There would be fun, fun, fun!

I couldn't wait to go. The Christmas before I asked and received a three-piece red vinyl luggage set. I was all ready to go. I was eight years old and I was ready for an adventure. The two weeks before, I set down with the itinerary list and started packing. My Zest soap, crest toothpaste, wash rag and towel, etc. I counted down the weeks, then the days. I was ready!

Mr. Minturn pulled up in a Wagoneer station wagon, tan with wood grain on the side. It had so many children and luggage in it. I thought for sure me and my new red over-niter and case wouldn't fit! I panicked! But somehow, we did. And my adventure began. Going to camp was all new to me and thinking back at the time it must've been hard for Mom and Dad to see me go. My Dad believed it was important for me to be independent and he encouraged me every step of the way. I remember him helping me pack and showing me how to fold my clothes. My enthusiasm must have been contagious.

When we arrived, there were lots of children. They were of all ages, from everywhere, even as far as Somerset. I was thrilled to meet new people. We went to our cabins and met our counselor. She was a pretty girl, maybe eighteen. Her name was Mary Ritchie. I still remember her name because I wrote her letters for years after that summer. We each had a bunk. I had never slept on a bunk, so I got one on top. I was elated!

After settling in they were having a get together for all the campers. A sort of get to know you time and have some refreshments: Kool aid and cookies. I still to this day love Kool aid and cookies. It was around a campfire and I loved that. As always there was a time when each camper stood up and gave their name, where they were from and a little testimonial. Some even sang little bible songs. Well I was ready. I had learned a new song. I would be a hit! I was antsy! Hurry! I wanted to sing! When it was my time, I stood up, very straight, told my name and began to sing." YOU ARE MY SUNSHINE, MY ONLY SUNSHINE," I sung the entire song not missing a beat.

When the service was over I was took aside and kindly and ever so gently told my song was not quite "appropriate"! I wasn't quite sure what Mrs.Wahlsted meant but I was sure I wouldn't be singing it again (not here anyways).

I enjoyed my camping experience and went many more times, seven to be exact! I learned a lot, but mostly I learned about the people. I love children and God! It is too bad we don't have them in our schools today!

Chapter 10
The Princess Dress

I was born and raised in South Eastern Kentucky at the foothills of the Appalachian Mountains. I had no concept that I was poor; I was the same as everyone else. My family, my cousins and our neighbors all lived pretty much the same way. We had plenty enough to eat, although not fancy! Maw and Paw kept us in milk, butter and eggs. They would kill a hog in the spring and fall, then meat would be plentiful. Hams for Easter and Christmas. Summertime we spent in the garden and late summer we "put up" what we grew. I wore hand me down clothes from my cousins. Sometimes Aunt Ruth would send her son, Jim's overalls. As Mom used to say, "Be thankful you have them, never mind they are boys'!" I didn't mind them to play in but I really wanted pretty things for school.

    Mommy got a Kenmore sewing machine from Sears when we were stationed in Newport

Rhode Island, It was her pride and joy. She was learning quite well on it, making curtains and such. But now she had decided she was adept enough to make me a dress! She had purchased a whole bundle of beautiful damask-like curtain material. It resembled a rose crème brocade! I was ecstatic! My new dress would be cut from this. I could hardly wait until it was made! She could make a pattern Aunt Zona taught her, but she could not put in a zipper, nor could she make a button hole.

When it was finished, it was so beautiful! The sleeves were leg of mutton, and the skirt resembled a ballerina's, and it fit like a glove! I couldn't wait to get to school to show off my new dress. Due to the fact it had no zipper, nor buttons, Mom said she would just tack it at the neck and waist with a slip stitch, no one would be the wiser. She tied a ribbon around my waist and off I went!

I began to itch on the bus and by the time I had gotten to school I was in full blown red hive state! I arrived at my second-grade class swelling, hives and tearing up. It didn't take Mrs. Bennett long to discover the problem. My dress was made out of fiberglass curtain material, and I was sewn in! Nothing was to be done, but to be returned home and redressed. I was so embarrassed! I am sure Mother was as embarrassed as me when Mr. Ball, the principal delivered me home with the instructions to bring me back with suitable school attire on.

Not being prepared she retrieved my cousin Jim's overalls. Already upset, that was the last thing I wanted to wear! I started to well up to cry and I looked at my Mother and sensed, you better not!

I sucked it up and went back to school. Not in my lovely princess dress, but in Jim's ole faded overalls. I hated to admit it but never did anything ever feel so good.

Chapter 11
Tobacco

My grandmother has been on my mind today! Rose Wilson was one of a kind, well I better take that back. She was from a lineage of women I am proud to be a part of! All strong, independent, hardworking and would fight a circle saw!

I have heard tales of my great grandmother Josephine and her mother the Cherokee Indian. All had tempers, loyalty and undying love for their people!

My Maw believed that if one was good more was better! Two such episodes come to mind today. My Maw was the go to childcare when we were small because as everyone knew you didn't leave your children with just "anybody". Back when I was growing up there was no childcare per se, no daycare, no babysitters. God forbid you would have strangers taking care of your little ones.

Aunt Shirley, my mother's youngest sister,

had decided to go to work at the "corset" factory in town to help make ends meet. Her son Dennis was two years younger than me and they lived near Maw by the church house. He was quite a docile little boy. You could characterize him as a "follower". I on the other hand was nicknamed "ole tear'em up!". I still don't know why!

    On one such fall day my Maw had us both. Old southern women did not smoke, well not in public! But they did dip snuff and some chewed tobacco. My Maw did both! Sitting on her porch peeling apples to dry both Dennis and I were fascinated with the chewing tobacco! Me not so much, I really wanted to smoke! First it was me, I jumped in head first! I wanted to smoke. She wasn't quite sure. But she would let me try 'rabbit' tobacco! Now what rabbit tobacco was I have no clue. But it grew wild and in the fall, it was dry! You stripped it from the stalk and rolled it in brown paper bag and licked the edges shut just like the other 'banned' substance I am loathing to mention. You smoke it just like a cigarette. Well I felt ten feet tall sitting on Maw's porch puffing on my 'rabbit' tobacco cigarette. That is for about the first hour and a half, because she kept rolling and I kept smoking! I must have been the color of a frog pond when my mother came to get me. I know my head was spinning and I don't believe I have ever been that sick in my life! If you think I was sick Den was worse, he ate a whole plug of Days Work! Shirley about died! She quit work that day and never went back!! She told me years later she told Maw, "You are going to kill my baby!" Maw said as only she could "Ah Shirley, a good worming is good for the boy! He's a little too wiry!" That was my Maw.

***

It's four in the morning and I can't sleep. Memories are keeping me awake tonight. Writing about my Maw brings back all those memories that have been locked away for years.

She seemed like a big woman to me. She had big hands! You know the kind that are weather worn and tired, but are so adept at everything from cutting corn to wiping the smallest tears. She had the whitest of hair, wispy and cut short like mine. Once a month she would go to Flossie's and get a rinse. Sometimes it would be blue, sometimes it would be lilac! Whatever the mood hit! For the better part of her life she wore dresses with cotton hose rolled up on rubber bands at knee level. She was fifty - three when I was born! Old, I thought! She would rather be out than in! She tended the farm and made it go! Her Mammy (Grandmother) was Cherokee and from across Pine Mountain, and she had taught her about herbs and mountain medicine. She was a mid-wife and had birthed many babies.

When the "grands " stayed with her we had adventures! She would put on her big straw hat with the green plastic visor insert and tie it under her chin and gathered up what children would accompany her. My cousin Jim, I think went with her a lot, but sometimes Den and I got to go too. Hunting ginseng and yellow root. This time it was blackberry picking. In the '50s and '60s blackberries grew abundantly along fence rows and river bottoms. Maw made the best canned blackberries ever! Right now, I could drink a quart of the juice from some.

So, on this day me and Den would get to go! Maw put turpentine around my ankles and wrists to ward off the feared chiggers! But Den would have none of it! He didn't like the smell. Later he would wish he had held his breath. We had a fruitful day! Lots of big juicy berries! With the exception of a little red across my nose I was in good shape! Den not so much! He started digging and he dug and he dug and he dug!

He scratched until he started to cry! Well Den looked just like a 5-year-old Opie Taylor (red hair and all). And his privates had started to swell! He was ate up with chiggers, mostly in his lower extremities! When Aunt Shirley got home, Maw had him sitting in a galvanized tub of Epsom salts out back and he was crying to beat the band!

Needless to say, Shirley wasn't a happy camper! She scooped Den up and took him to the emergency room. My Maw seemed to think it was unnecessary. I heartily agreed! I thought she was handling it just fine, and told her so. At eight years old my Maw could do anything!

Chapter 12
Turtle Soup

There used to be an old wives' tale that if in any year there were more boys born than girls, there would be a war. Well, it must've been so, for the year I was born, 1956, very few girls were born (in my neighborhood anyway). I remember well, there was Larry Logan, Larry Reynolds, Derwin Mckiddy, Marty Jackson and Roy Lambdin, just to name a few. I was older than them all, but just by a few days. They were my playmates on a daily basis, and sometimes my cousin Den. At eight and nine years old, hierarchy is very much sought after and even though I was older I was still just the girl. But I had been under tutelage of my elder cousins Lynn and Jim Mays, and I knew everything!

    A little insight, I learned to collect all sorts of small creatures, mostly from the small creeks and riverbanks at their hands. We would get an old Maxwell House coffee can and fill it full of crawdads, salamanders, (the kind with the red dots on their backs), frogs, garter snakes and terrapins (turtles). Behind my house in various sizes of mason jars was a menagerie of animals and bugs, some alive, some dead! Some in alcohol and some with holes punched in the lids. My prize was two rubbery black snake eggs stored in alcohol for all posterity. I was a budding scientist then.

I lived across the road from a tributary of the Cumberland River (Poplar Creek). Back then it was beautiful and clean. There was a shackled walking bridge across it. In places it was shallow and others it was really deep. We knew the difference. On this day the boys wanted to fish and I wanted to prowl. Along the riverbank was where the good specimens were. Now this is where the tale gets a little, how should we say it, murky.

Now, Larry Reynolds was a sweet little boy, a follower. Larry Logan and I got him in trouble more times than I can remember. Now I am one week older than Larry, so I have the upper hand. Next, you need to know he was scared of everything. I had to bait his hook (with Bologna). It was said I was the one who found the turtle, chased him with it and dared him to pick it up! But I don't rightly remember it just that way. Anyhow, even with my vast reptilian knowledge at eight years old, I somehow missed the lesson on mud turtles versus terrapin! That sucker latched on to Larry and wouldn't let go! He was screaming at me yelling "LET ME SEE, LET ME SEE!" Finally, we got him over to Larry Logan's dad and he had to use plyers to release the jaws of that beast. It left a place as Maw used to say. After that Larry wasn't allowed to play with me again for a very long time.

TURTLE SOUP (WORKS JUST AS Good for oyster or any fish)
1 1/2 sticks of butter
2 1/2 pounds' turtle meat
salt and pepper
2 med onions
6 stalks of celery
30 cloves garlic minced
3 bell peppers diced
1 tbsp. thyme grd
1 tbsp. oregano grd
4 bay leaves
2 quarts' beef stock
1 cup flour
1 tbsp. hot pepper sauce
26 oz. dry sherry optional

1/4 cup Worcestershire
2 large lemons
3 cups tomatoes, chopped, seeded and peeled (or a large can)
10 oz. fresh spinach (or a bag of frozen)

DIRECTIONS;
Brown turtle meat in large pot with half stick of butter. Season with salt and pepper, add onions and celery, garlic and peppers. Constantly stirring add your herbs and sauté for about 20 minutes. Add stock. In a saucepan make a roux using the remaining butter and flour, slowly adding it to the melting flour not allowing it to burn. Cook it for about 3 minutes, until it is the consistency of sand. Add this to the stock a little at a time stirring with a whisk until it has all been added to the soup. It will need to simmer for a couple of hours. The Worcestershire sauce, tomatoes, and spinach can be added now.

Chapter 13
Golden's Creek

The weekends that I got to ride the bus to Golden's Creek was always an adventure. I packed my clothes in a big brown paper bag and anticipated the ride all day. I stared out the big school windows and glanced at the big, black, round-faced clock. As its hands slowly moved toward three o'clock I raced toward my bus. More times than not I was drawn back by the scruff of my neck and admonished to walk not run making me late and having to take a seat in the back of the bus. Away from my girlfriends.

    As the bus turned up the creek my anticipation grew, I could not wait to get out of my school clothes and into my overalls and begin what would be a glorious weekend. We were going to burn off the old hillside and maybe just maybe, get to ride on the tractor with my cousin Jim. I raised up in the seat and hung my head out the window soaking up the smell of the new fall day and got my nostrils full of dust from the gravel road. It felt good. A little grit in your craw never hurt anybody, my Maw used to say. I'm sure I must have a ton of it.

When we got to Maw's Jim and Lynn got off too. I was ecstatic, the more the merrier. For Maw us grands were free labor, for us it was adventure land. Maw and Paw lived on a hill. Their driveway circled around the hillside that was circumvented by a barbwire fence. By the end of the summer it would be overgrown with blackberry briars, poke berries, and weeds of all sorts. There were no weed eaters back then, so in the fall they would burn the fence row after the first major frost as they were dead and dry. My cousin Jim was always allowed the great privilege of tending the fire. I, who felt a great need to do so, was not allowed. I was too young and not adept. I cringe as I think of it yet. Maw would stand with hoe or mattock in hand and me in Jim's hand-me down jeans just itching to get to that fire. The bank beneath the fence row was steep and there was a deep ditch below it, before the gravel driveway. Just shy of the driveway was a stack of what appeared to be old rotted logs, I had an epiphany! I could burn them!

Maw had moved on down around the hill to help Jim. So, I retrieved Paw's red metal kerosene can and doused the pile of timbers and proceeded to use Maw's kitchen matches to lite the wood. It burnt slowly at first but then the dry wood took off and BOOM! My face felt hot as my eyelashes and eyebrows were singed along with my bangs. I could smell burnt hair. Apparently, my Maw could hear the boom from around the hill as she came running. I ran as fast as I could and she scooped me up asking if I was hurt. Again, she was so glad I wasn't, it was my saving grace. I was not whipped that day but I made up for it many times after.

I found out later the timber wood I burnt was not as old and rotted as I thought. It was hickory posts that Paw had saved to use in the bottoms to divide the fields to keep the cattle out of the hay fields. He was livid! Hickory fence posts were expensive and I had burnt over a hundred of them. Not one word did he say to me but he said plenty to Maw. I can still feel her big old arms around me as she scooped me up, she was trembling. Even though she never said so, I know she thought she was to blame.

For the better part of my third-grade year I didn't have any eyebrows or eyelashes or bangs for that matter. She got up the mornings I stayed with her and got out her red Maybelline eye pencil and drew me some on. I thought I looked swell, my third-grade pictures are priceless. I had the best eyebrows in class!

Chapter 14
Cinnamon Rolls

This morning I was in IGA and passed the cinnamon rolls. Now, I am a diabetic and they are not in my basic food choices. It has been many years since I have imbibed, but there was a time.

In 1963 my Dad was in the V.A. hospital in Louisville for testing, and my Maw was again taking care of my sister and me. This time, in our own home in Paul's Town on highway ninety-two. As I said before, my Maw was a great proponent of "if some is good, more is better!" We lived twenty – one miles from any substantial town (Pineville, Williamsburg or Barbourville).

So, to accommodate rural areas there was a rolling store. That had necessities as well as some luxuries. It was an old Ford school bus painted red! When it came by it was always so exciting! There would be food and snacks, but sometimes coloring books and small dolls in clear plastic bags hung by hooks on the walls. My Maw couldn't (wouldn't) drive, so she enjoyed the shopping too. This day when the big red bus pulled up, we all made a bee line to it! After she made her purchases she saw me perusing the cinnamon rolls with their heavy sugary coating! "Deb do you want some of them cakes", she said. I shook my head fast! "Give me two" Maw said. I was overjoyed!

When we returned home I proceeded to devour one. "Honey do you want another? Eat all you want!", Maw said. It was like music to my ears! I literally began to inhale two packages of cinnamon rolls! Well by about six o'clock that night, I began to get nauseated and then shortly after my color drained to a chalky white and the room began to spin! I held it as long as I could. I am not a big fan of up chucking and I fight it tooth and nail. But this time it won. My room, my bed, my clothes were covered in cinnamon rolls! My Maw, woman of the hour took over!! She never said a bad word, Thank God!

So, today as I look at that package of cinnamon rolls, I think, not in a million years!

Chapter 15
Labor Day

Labor Day weekend in the south always means family get togethers with out of towners coming in and staying over! In the early 1960's most of southeast Kentucky was dry! In other words, you could not buy or imbibe in public alcoholic beverages of any sort! Well, my disenfranchised family on my Father's side were from Cleveland, Ohio. A hotbed of sin and to hear my Maw tell it the Jezebel of Babylon was coming (my Dad's sister Ruby). I on the other hand thought she hung the moon. She and her husband owned a bar. "SHAMEFUL," my Maw would say. And on top of that her husband was a "SHADY" character. For example: One year for Christmas I wanted a mini bike and we couldn't afford one but Aunt Ruby brought me one! I was elated until Daddy wouldn't let me have it! I didn't understand! He said, " Because it fell off a truck!" Years later I found out what that meant!

Aunt Ruby was beautiful! She had platinum blonde hair and it was teased in a bouffant up do! She wore eyeliner and blue eye shadow. She had her nails done, and they had a big black Lincoln car with a phone in it. The first one I had ever seen! She had a little orange Pomeranian dog. The first one of them I ever saw too.

My father wasn't always a Baptist! He was converted to religion early on by the Catholics. He believed there was good in all faiths and that whatever church you were near God was present there. So, the part about imbibing alcoholic beverages was not necessarily present in the ten commandments so therefore God must not have thought it to be too important! Mother on the other hand thought differently. I suspect that is one of the great differences between the Catholics and the Baptists!

The Saturday night before the Sunday of Labor Day weekend 1963 Aunt Ruby, Uncle Joe and Daddy and Mommy had set up late to play cards and visit. Some beverages were provided and served by the house guests as appropriate gifts. Our house was fairly new and not altogether finished. The carport had a block wall across the front but nothing else. Upon arising and finding everyone asleep after a late night of card playing and imbibing maybe a little too much, I investigated the bright and colorful bottles sitting around. They proved too delightful for words. By now Tami was up too. To keep from making too much noise I stealth fully moved one by one the pretty bottles and set them across the cement blocks on the front of the house toward highway ninety-two. There were just enough to go from one side to another: Crown Royal, Blue Nun, and more.

    Well, I must elaborate. To get to our church Old Poplar Creek Baptist Church you must pass my house! This Sunday morning my Maw and Paw passed by and saw what appeared to be every type of liquor known to man standing on my carport and me not at Sunday Schoo. THE #$%& HIT THE FAN! When church was over my Maw made a pit stop at my house! I don't remember who was the maddest Mom, Dad, or Maw, but I couldn't sit down for a week! Until this day I can't stand to look at Blue Nun.

Chapter 16
The Lady Schick

A couple of weeks ago my friend Ida and I visited Henderson Settlement! We went especially for the junk store. I saw an item that I almost bought not because I needed it, but for sentimental reasons. A lady Schick Razor! Now at my age I don't have enough hair on my body to even worry about, much less purchase a razor for, but this was for my sister Tami as a "remember when!"

In the summer of 1971, the year Mom married Chester, at fifteen I was exploring my new-found womanhood. Shaving my legs was one of them! Back then there was only "SAFETY RAZORS". I really don't know what there was "safe" about them! Every time I used them I almost cut my ankles off. So, Mom, distrusting my ability with the "safety razor" allowed me to use her new Lady Schick.

In the early 70's new products were coming along every day. My favorite was QT, short for

Quick Tan! It was the predecessor to these new self-tanners we have now, but, well let's say, much worse! For a novice you could turn orange. Really orange, and it wouldn't come off! It had to wear off, and if you didn't shave you looked like an orange cat; all furry and orange. I would know!

Well on one such Friday night I was preparing for a big weekend, but I was to babysit Tami and Joyce as Mom and Chester went out to eat. No problem. I HAD A PLAN! We would shave our legs, apply the QT and have a girls' night! No problem. Everything was going on schedule.

Now let me give you some insight on my sister Tami. She was nine years old and at that time and a little whinny. She had a habit of putting the ends of her hair in her mouth or for that matter anything else; pencils, pens, etc. That night it was the end of the cord of the Lady Schick Razor. I had unplugged the razor from the cord (leaving it plugged in) and left it laying on the bed. Why she did something like that is beyond me! Joyce and I were busy applying our QT when all of a sudden, we heard this bloodcurdling scream! I saw the cord locked to her tongue! She had apparently stuck her tongue in the little holes and it had got her!

I grabbed for it but it wouldn't let go! Thank God for Joyce as she reached for the cord and unplugged it. I told you she was older than her years! Tami fell back on the bed! I thought for sure she was dead! Her face white as a sheet. Jo brought a wet wash rag and we washed her face. Now you need to know, I am sure it was a traumatic experience, but my sister has the drama queen down to a science.

I know I owe her for making her have her playhouse in the outhouse, or for leaving her Thumbelina doll out in the rain and ruining it, or for tearing her paper doll's heads off, but this time, no – I did not tell her to stick her tongue in an electric cord! But who got in trouble? Yours truly. My Adventure in babysitting expired that night, for a while anyway. She played it to the hilt!

When Mom came home she was still laying prone on the bed, rag on her head and tongue lulled out! My mother almost had a cardiac on the spot! I thought, a little jolt didn't hurt. I had more than that when I tried to rewire my record player. Mother never raised her voice to her, but I sure got a tongue lashing! After it was all over I don't think she put too many things in her mouth, and I don't think the Lady Schick ever worked the same again.

Chapter 17
The Wake

Last week Brother Arnold Petrey was laid to rest. They told me it was a sight at the people who came to the visitation and later to the funeral. Croley Funeral Home always does a fine job. I am a bit prejudiced as they are family. For close to a hundred years they have been putting people away. One time I remember quite well, when I was growing up, a funeral and a wake was an event. Like a birth or a wedding, it culminated your passing! My family, like most southern families, drew it out over days and sometimes, if you had family up North, a week!

If you were a man and a Mason you would have a separate service too. A woman would have an Eastern Star service. Family would descend from all over bringing children that had probably never met the deceased, but would come out of respect. The wake consisted of food, and lots of it, brought in by family and friends. Churches, no matter the denomination, furnished chairs for the mourners and the funeral home sometimes set up tents in the yard if the house was too small. This wake was for some of "Chalk" Lambdin's people on Golden's Creek. Croley's had come and set up the body in the "front" room (it wasn't called a living room back then because usually it had a bed in it). My Aunt Ruth lived just across and down the road from them. Aunt Ruth and Uncle Clyde owned all the fields and bottom lands below the road. It had been divided by fence rows to keep the cows away from the corn.

Now let me tell you about my cousin Donna "Lynn". She is the oldest "grand" and the sister to my cousin Jim. She was about thirteen years old at the time. She had auburn hair, freckles and a slight overbite. Earlier in the summer she had broken her nose by jumping off a two-story barn with a sheet playing "RIPCORD"! She was a daredevil. All I ever knew, I learned from her. I followed her around like she was The Queen of Sheba. She could do anything, and would!

On this night Aunt Ruth was attending this wake. Most of the neighborhood came. The house was overflowing into the yard. People were milling about drinking coffee and talking softly to themselves. All of a sudden, voices raised and people began rushing to the porch to see the commotion, Aunt Ruth too. Upon getting to the porch she saw Lynn with a teal green chenille housecoat on, jumping her pinto pony barebacked over the fence rows putting on a show for the mourners. Aunt Ruth was beyond embarrassed. She was livid. She pulled her black patent leather pocketbook high under her arm and started down that walk with the stature of a drill sergeant and as she did she broke off a long slim limb of the willow tree. I knew what that meant. Lynn took one final turn and made a curtain call to her audience. I guess she figured she might as well go down kicking. I think of it yet and can see her bent low on that pony with her hair flailing in the wind! What a sight; What a memory!

Chapter 18
Hugh Charles

Maw's house on the hill consisted of only five rooms. The front room, a bedroom, a kitchen, a dining room, and a loft. There was no bathroom when I was growing up. It was added, later on, to the back porch. Sometime after I married and Brent was born in 1975. I always wondered how they raised five children in that house. It was probably less than a thousand square feet. The size of my family room.

When I was growing up all the grandchildren slept upstairs in the loft. It had an old rope bed with a feather mattress on it. In the summer it was hot, in the winter it was cold. We would cover up with Maw's quilts, all handmade. Mostly out of the children's worn out clothes. A few crazy quilts made out of Paw's old suit coats. They were so heavy you could barely turnover. God forbid if your bedmate was a bed wetter! There was a window on each eave of the house and the bed set beneath it. As the breeze carried up the creek in the fall and spring, it was Heaven. And at night the sounds were a cacophony of frogs and owls and any number of night creatures.

As I laid in Maw's soft bed, smelling of sunshine and lye soap, I would dream of all the things I would do and be. She often would tell me how smart I was and how my great – great – Grandmother had outlived the civil war, when the Yankees had stormed their home taking all of their food and leaving them with nothing to eat while facing a bad, cold winter. My Grandmother, or GG, had known about herbs and roots and berries and how to make coffee from bark. Maw told me I could survive too. During those days I would go with her, she with her hoe or mattock, and her straw hat. And we would scour the mountains for berries and roots and herbs. When my Daddy got sick she made yellow root tea for him to drink to clear his kidneys.

As time went by I drew on the strength she gave me those days. When I was young and learning. Today I wish for those days again, those days of innocence. For me as well as her. In 1964 her world would turn upside down and life would never be the same. In four months my Maw, as I knew her, would be lost forever.

My uncle HC, Hugh Charles, was young and vibrant, and handsome. He was tall, dark haired like Mom, with the look of a young George Hamilton. He had the most vivacious laugh and could lite up any room. You just wanted to be in his presence. In 1964 he had joined the National Guard to ward off the awful draft and the uncertainty of the Vietnam conflict. Boys from our community were already returning in boxes. Some in body bags, families unsure if it was even them. So, HC was sent to Fort Knox. Close enough to come home if Maw and Paw needed him. He had married the previous year to one of my Davis cousins, and they had a baby that was just learning to walk.

    HC came home for Easter and had a horrible toothache. So, Maw took him to have it pulled. It never stopped bleeding. She took him to our family doctor. The prognosis was not good, Non-Hodgkin's Lymphoma. It was very aggressive. The doctor sent him to the University of Kentucky in Lexington some one hundred miles away. At that time, we had no interstate highways and our roads were two lanes and some treacherous for wrecks.

    For the next four months it was a continuous stream of blood transfusions and chemotherapy. HC lost his beautiful black hair and the last pictures we had of him were taken at a local theme park standing between my mother and daddy. His bald head gleaming; his smile was as wide as ever. Our extended family, then big, from as far as Detroit drove to Lexington to give blood. Hoping to spare his life to no avail. In October he lost his battle, he was twenty-four. My MAW was devastated. She was never the same again.

    I have often heard that it was never meant for parents to bury their children. I understand why. In later years I saw a picture of my Maw at HC's grave. She was the same age I am now, but she looked so much older. She grieved until she died, for more than thirty years.

***

One story of HC and Maw my Aunt Shirley used to tell long after they were both gone always makes me smile. As it gives a flavor as the relationship between them and why she loved him so. HC was Maw's youngest son and at the time of this story around eleven or twelve. Maw, an avid storyteller, sometimes embellished her stories to make them more dramatic or to add a little gossip. This time HC took umbrage and told her so.
"That wasn't how it was", he told Maw.

"Well, I reckon it was", she said.

"No, it wasn't, have it! I don't want it," he said, ever so nonchalantly arched against the porch post.

Before long they were both laughing and Maw knew HC had got the best out of the debate. He always did. I look back and I know where my son got his lawyering skills.

Chapter 19
Breakfast

Breakfast was always the biggest meal of the day. Paw worked in the mines and they were used to rising at four am. So even later in life they still kept their routine. At around four or five in the morning I would be greeted with the smell of freshly ground boiled coffee and frying meat: sausage, bacon, pork tenderloin, or chicken or any two or three. It depended on how many of us grands were there.

    My Maw didn't particularly like to cook, but breakfast was the one exception. She loved it. Her kitchen was the closed in back porch, it had two stoves. One was an old-fashioned wood burning cook stove, and the other a gas stove, fueled by propane. She had an old Frigidaire refrigerator that must have been fifty years old when I was a child. It was so small it barely held milk and eggs and the freezer was the size of a shoe box. In the middle of her kitchen was a big old table covered in an oil cloth that had red squares with grapes and other fruit on it. She would sit a big bowl of flour on the table, add a handful of Fishers lard and her big hands would deftly throw out a pan full of the most beautiful fluffy tasty "cathead" biscuits you had ever ate.

I don't think she ever changed the flour in that big old bowl. It was huge. I wish I had it now. She would call us down from upstairs to eat. She never had to call us more than once. We couldn't wait to sit at her table and eat. I learned to drink coffee under her tutelage. Strong, Eight O'clock coffee. Boiled thick resembling a thin syrup. She would pour it in a saucer and lace it with sugar and cream, the kind reamed from fresh milk, not the kind you get from a carton in the store. For years I never could drink milk from stores. It seemed so diluted, so thin. Not like milk at all. My Maw used to say, if I had to drink that all the time I would just give up. I know now that was why I was so alert and why my teachers had so much trouble keeping my attention. two or three cups of my Maw's coffee was sure to have done it.

Lunch was usually some kind of bean, pinto, green, lima and corn bread and a meat, usually chicken, as we had plenty of it. This was never a problem, until my sister became attached to one of Maw's chickens. In the spring the chickens have little doodlers, little chicks. When they are handled at an early age they become like pets. My sister loved them. Sometimes the mother chickens can be mean and not let you near them but this mother hen was very docile and didn't mind Tami playing with her chicks. My sister was little more than a toddler herself and when she was in the yard the little doodlers always trailed behind her. She could scoop them up and pet them like a kitten. They began to grow, very fast. Soon they were fryer size, but still they were Tami's pets. One by one they began to come up missing, until soon there was only one. By then Tami had named him. I think my Maw felt bad about frying him, so he lived longer and became a rooster. He was quite beautiful but as there was already a rooster among Maw's chickens he was short lived.

One day he came up missing too. I remember my sister crying and crying, and I remember my Maw holding her close and telling her that her chicken had went to Heaven. To a toddler that was something hard to understand. She told her how beautiful it was, with big colorful flowers and sunshine all day long and other chickens for him to play with and that one day she would see him again. I saw my sister look into her face and the tears stop. A smile crossed her little face as she envisioned such a place and she put her arms around my Maw's neck and I knew my MAW was just as hurt as my sister. I saw the tears in her eyes too. Never again were we allowed to play with the chickens.

***

I think Gary Helton is trying to kill me! Every weekend morning the waft of fresh coffee and bacon frying permeates my house! The dogs awaken with whines and whimpers, and me to that awful gnawing in the pit of your stomach that says, "feed me"! Gary is my tenant. He rents my basement apartment and is no doubt the best cook ever, His Twinkie cake is to die for. He is an appliance repairman but on the weekends, he cooks. He could make an old shoe taste good! Any opportunity to have folks over and roll out the smoker, he finds it – Easter, Fourth of July, Hanukah, etc.! He can smoke anything, chicken, pork tenderloin, even turtle! If he can smoke it, I can eat it! He always shares! Never does he forget to bring a plate with a little (lot) of everything. Don't tell him but I would almost give him free rent! ARGH! Being a diabetic has its drawbacks.

Sometimes you can see and smell but not eat! Awful! Food has been, to me anyway, my means of sustenance: Social, physical and otherwise!

Gary was a Godsend. He came to me when I was at my wits end and my pocketbook was too. Shortly after I built my house my finances went south in 2006. Like everyone else during the housing boom, I built more than I needed and it caught up with me. And I put my house up for sale.

Gary showed up one bright sunny day in his old, white, Ford utility van, wanting to know what I wanted for my house. When I told him what I had to have it was quite a shock, but he took a tour anyway. After looking over the basement, he stood back and cocked his head, rubbing his chin, he stated unequivocally that it would make a lovely apartment! I looked at him and back at the room and agreed that it would.

"How much do you think it would take?", he said.

"About $2000 I should think," I said.

"And how long,".

"At least three months", I countered.

"I'll take it!". He said.

And that is how he came to be my neighbor and

good friend. We have endured his divorce, my heart attack and the loss of my Sami (my Shitzu of fourteen years) And the birth of his new baby Addison.

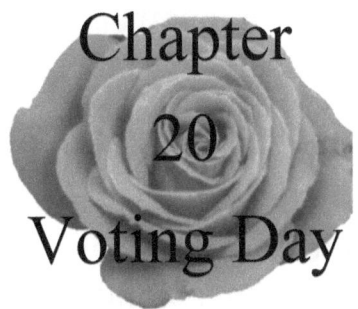

Chapter 20
Voting Day

My Maw would and could fight a circle saw! Of all the lessons she taught me, the most important was that the right to vote was a God given privilege!

My Maw worked as an election officer for as long as I could remember! She was very "political" when I was growing up. She defined an independent woman. All her sisters were independent minded too. I am, who I am, because of her. I remember Maw and me sitting and breaking up beans discussing the importance of voting! "We were no more than cattle" she once said! "They were treated better!!".

I always remembered what she said. She told me horror stories of widows, being thrown off family farms when the husband died and of mining widows being kicked out of mining camp houses because their husband had been killed in the mine. She told of women not being able to own things in their name or being able to go to the bank without their husbands. These things I still ponder today. She was so proud to be able to walk in that polling booth and cast her first vote! I remember wanting to do the same thing.

Elections used to be an event. It was talked about and argued about months in advance. My Maw was just such a person, and me eight years old, relished the chance to be in the middle of it all!

My Maw could not take part in any electioneering, as she was an election officer, but that didn't keep me from it! There was somebody running that Maw was especially interested in. So, she gave me a whole dollar, to stand outside the polls and hand out cards for this person.

I was so excited. I got up early that morning, as we had to be there by six. Maw fixed her big breakfast. I would sip my coffee from a saucer and eat biscuits and gravy. Then she would get her headscarf, tying it under her chin, her big black pocketbook and hike it up under her arm and then we were off!

Paw drove us in his ole black '56 Chevy truck. He wore his Sunday overalls and white starched shirt with his grey felt fedora. I felt so important. Maw went in, leaving me to electioneer! In those days' vote buying consisted of swapping liquor for votes or they would "pay" you to haul voters! Either way the man with the most money won! I began handing out cards and talking about the finer points that this candidate had, parroting my Maw. It wasn't long before a highly intoxicated voter arrived and proceeded to question me on my candidate's qualifications! I bantered back and forth until finally I said, "well Maw said if he gets elected Uncle Raleigh will get a job on the county road crew!" My Maw must've been listening because she swooped down, got me and took me to a place where I would electioneer no more!

    Thinking back, it is a wonder she ever let me go with her again, but she did and I remember the first vote I got to cast. I will never take for granted the opportunity to vote! Thank you, Maw!

Chapter 21
The Sweepstakes

Last night I was reminded of something that happened when I was a small child, or let us say a youngster. Saturday night me and Ida Gaddis went out to eat, of course eating was included, at Cheddar's and I wanted to stop and check out the mini-RV'S. My new goal in life is to own one of these and hook it to my little VW Beetle, with dogs in tow and crisscross this nation visiting all the places I have once lived. Stopping to see new and old friends alike. Great idea huh? This goal is not necessarily new to me, I was reminded, by a dear cousin last night.

    Some years ago, let's say forty some odd, I was this precocious young girl fascinated with getting mail. I filled out everything coming and going just to get something with my name on it delivered by U.S. mail. Just like now it didn't take long before I was getting Publisher's Clearing House Sweepstakes, and Readers Digest and other's too numerous to count. One such contest sent me a check for $1000,000. I think years later they did the same thing and some fool actually cashed it! What bank did that is beyond me? The sweepstakes people asked questions like, what kind of car would you like? What kind of house? And on this date where could we pick you up in our limousine? Well any ordinary person would not have fell for that but I did hook line and sinker! I ordered their magazines! And told my cousins Debbie, Billy and Johnny Fulton that we were going to be rich and have an adventure. It was all true I had their check to prove it.

    For days we lay and plotted and planned what we were going to buy and where we were going to go when the man came in the limousine. Our mothers were not going to tell us what to do anymore! It was a plan. The day came I packed my "grip". I put on my Sunday clothes and I waited. At about dusky dark Joie Fulton, Debbie, Billy and Johnny's mother called fuming! She wanted to know what I concocted for her children? They were sitting out by the road with their bags packed refusing to come in and eat supper with some crazy story about a man in a limousine coming to get them! The wrath of my mother came down on me hard! I still had my check. Old dreams die hard, and so do the bills for Reader's Digest.

Chapter 22
Military Funeral

I read something today that brought back sad memories! In March of 1968 we were in the midst of a war not of our own choosing, not unlike today. There were 766 Kentuckians to die unnecessarily in that war. One was my cousin McKenley Odis Matlock, twenty-five years old, married father of one with one on the way. It would never know its father!

    I was twelve years old. My father was thirty-five. It was one of the few times I ever saw him cry. My Father was brought up pretty much an orphan. His mother died when he was four years old shortly after childbirth. He had two older siblings and a younger brother. Their father was, what you might say, a drunk, and they were tossed from relative to relative. My father once told me a story of being so cold he took a little wagon and went along the railroad tracks and picked up coal to keep warm. At seven years old his father put a paper tag on him and shipped him off to his Uncle's in West

Virginia on a bus! My father treasured the families who cared for him when he was small and the children he grew up with! Ken was one of them.

In 1968 McKenley Odis Matlock was killed in Vietnam. I never knew the specifics of his death but I knew the consequences. His parents were Amon and Clara Matlock; she was my Father's cousin. They had a house full of children and also, they had a houseful of love, and when Ken died it was devastating to them all. Southern families are close, real close! A wake was held at home, food was brought in and prepared by good Christian ladies, the casket was set up with pink torchers placed at the head and foot. They cast a pink glow over the bronze casket. Two Marines stood guard respectfully!

All night the wake wore on and strong coffee was poured, as well as clear liquid from mason jars out back. The good Christian ladies tried ever so hard to get the servicemen to sit down in straight back chairs for "just a minute", but they kindly refused. Never leaving for a second their comrade.

The next day we all made the trek to the church, then the cemetery where I saw my first military funeral. Even at twelve years old, it caused my heart to leap as the rifles blared across the hills on that cold March day. I looked up as they were handing Ken's wife the flag that had been draped across the casket and saw the tears streaming down my Father's face.

    I did not know in little less than two years I would be standing on that same hillside with my mother accepting a flag for my father.

Chapter 23
Aunt Vinia

There are days in our lives when we experience immense joy and others sadness that is so intense that is indescribable. For those days I am forever grateful of the love my Maw taught me. In the spring and summer of 1963 I was eight years old and I was beginning to see the world not as a child, but as one of God's children. This was the year I accepted Jesus Christ as my savior. At Big Poplar Creek Baptist Church, my Daddy was a secretary there. My great Aunt Vinia Reynolds had wanted him to be a Deacon but he declined. It was a day I would always remember.

    We lived just around the curve at Paul's Town from Aunt Vinia and Uncle Bud, my Maw's only brother. She had come to our house to ask Daddy if he would take a position as one of the Deacons, because one of the elders had passed away. I can still see my Daddy. He would always take his fingers and run them through his thinning hair from his forehead to the back, when he would ponder something hard. And this day, this question seemed one he has a hard time telling my aunt no to. Not because he didn't know the answer, but because she was so insistent. As she kept giving him reasons why he should take the position, he finally raised his hand and gave her only one reason why he could not. "Vinia, he said. "The word says as a Deacon I must be head of my house and I am not. Me and Arlone are joint. We do not always agree on everything. Sometimes she is, sometimes I am. We do not have one over the other. This is not what God wanted." My Daddy said nothing else and my aunt left. A short time later, on a Sunday night at the same church, I walked down the aisle while Reverend Wade Partin gave an altar call and I gave my heart to the Lord. I can hardly remember my baptism. But I do remember how happy my Maw was. She had done what God had intended, to impart her faith to her family and in turn I would do the same. As a child I am not sure I was truly aware of how important that day was, but I know it changed my life forever. I do know it changed the way I described who I would tell people I was. I was a Christian forever and ever. I can remember my Maw being so pleased. She knew from that day forward I would be alright, and I was.

Chapter 24
The Swimming Pool

Summer is almost gone! Memories of summers before come flooding back; one specifically. Last night I had dinner with my sister Joyce. It was so good seeing her again since she moved away. We became sisters October 1, 1971 when my mother married her father, both were widowers. She was exactly nine months to the day younger than my sister Tami. But she seemed older. We "clicked" right from the start. She was easy to get along with. Tami and me, sometimes, more times than not, clashed.

    The following summer Chester, my step dad, and Mom decided to get us a pool. It would help solidify our family and pacify me. As I was slowly making new friends, this definitely helped. It was a four-foot-high by twenty-four inches round, above ground pool from Sears. When it came it was like Christmas! We thought it could be put up in one evening! WRONG! After that debacle, the quandary of filling up a pool that size, from a well was another hurdle to cross. Chester made a rule, to save the well pump, it must only run a slight drizzle! Oh No! All this time waiting and to endure this measly stream of water. I had a plan!

After a week, we only had, maybe eighteen inches of water, we would take our rafts, and float anyway. Each time Chester left, we would run, and turn it up, full on! Sounded good to us girls! Mom and Chester were gone to work all day and Chester's dad, John Dad, watched us. Now John Dad was old in my thinking! He was maybe seventy. He was kind and soft spoken and no match for three teen age girls! We donned our bikinis and slathered up in Copper tone oil, No SPF! I think I once used motor oil and iodine! We got on our rafts at break of day, and at noon, John Dad came out and tried to get us to come in and eat. "No", I said. "But we will take a pop and chips!" For the next four hours, we floated around in eighteen inches of water, with the sun, reflecting off the sides of the pool.

When Mom and Chester came home they made us get out! Not only did we look like lobsters Me and Jo had the hair of leprechauns! We had been bleaching our hair blonde and the chlorine in the pool was too strong. So now our hair was green! We looked like the Italian flag! All red and green! That wasn't the half of it! Our newly formed bosoms had produced giant pillows of clear fluid that ran across their tops! We were a walking billboard of what not to do. For days we walked around with our arms out stretched not touching our bodies covered in Noxema! We peeled! We scratched! We bonded! We laughed! We still do! It was torture then, it is fond memories now! And like it was meant to do, it made a family!

Chapter 25
The Car Wreck

For Milton Dunaway

What young girls will do for the "love" of a young man is sometimes devastating! For me it just about cost me my life. In the summer of 1972 I had just turned sixteen years old, and like every teenager I wanted a car. That year the big thing was the Chevy Nova. Everyone that was anyone had one. Conley Mills had the fanciest one in town! It was candy apple red with metal flake and a black vinyl top. It was an SS model with bucket seats and Crager wheels. It roared when it went around the square. Someone else had a robin egg blue just like it! Sharp! It was my dream car!

Well my mother had an alternative reason to buy me a car! Band practice, majorette practice, ball games, etc. I was running her to death. So, when I got my car I was on cloud nine! It wasn't exactly what I was expecting. It was a Nova alright, but it was frog pond green! It had hub caps, no fancy wheels, no 8-track player, AM radio only, and bench checked vinyl seats. No carpet either, plastic! I could've cared less! It was a car! Wheels! I was now free! I wasn't allowed free access to it. I had to beg and plead to get to drive and it had to be a good reason!

On this day Mom was going to Begley Drug to get a medicine refill. Ah Ha!! Joyce and I needed hair dye so we would go for her! After some cajoling she relented! I had a plan! Summer school was in session and a certain young man was working as an aide at GR Hampton. On our way to town I would just drop by and show him my new ride and how well I could drive. Bill Phipps was his name. Upon visiting with him, he asked if I could drive him home. It would be so much better than riding the bus! Me, never thinking twice, agreed!

Well, those of you who know, Smokey is quite a distance from downtown Barbourville and a little tricky for a new driver, and to beat it all, it had started to drizzle rain! Joyce Ann was always easy to get along with so that was why she always got to go with me! When we got to town I let her out with instructions to get Mom's meds and the hair dye and I would be back shortly! Oh yeah!

Our trip was uneventful enough until my trip back! I had not counted on how long it would take, nor the rain, so I floored it, and when I did I lost it on a curve and flipped it! I have never been so afraid in my life. Death loomed in front of me like never before! I could see my Mother's face! I climbed out having peed all over myself. I was standing out in the rain by my poor destroyed car when my angel appeared. A black-haired woman with two children stopped and asked if she could be of assistance.

"No," I cried. "My mother is going to kill me."

" No she won't honey! She will be so glad you are not hurt!" the lady said.

"You don't know my mother," I said. She packed me up and took me back to Bill's house to call my Mother to tell her what had happened.

My angel, I later found out, was Milton Dunaway. I don't remember what she said to my mother, but I remember she didn't say three words all the way home! The car sat parked in its crumbled state for quite a while before she had it fixed. It didn't matter for I wasn't in any shape to crawl back under a wheel! Thank you, Milton!

Chapter 26
Tom T Hall

For Sharon Reeves Cole

This afternoon on my way to work I heard a song by Tom T. Hall. Old dogs, children and watermelon wine! What memories it brought back! I felt a tear fall slowly down my cheek, as my chest tightened and my throat got too thick to breathe.

In 1971 I came to Knox County, a skinny fifteen-year-old, and not too pleased about it. My mother had remarried Chester Bryant, widower who also had two children. One, a grown married son named Wayne, and Joyce, ten, who was nine months to the day younger than my sister Tami. Coming from one county over and not knowing anyone, I was miserable. I had been with all my cousins and neighbors for most of my life and now I was lost.

The first time I saw him he was on the school bus. In 1971 everyone didn't drive to school. Gas was $.39 a gallon. Too high to gallivant around when a very good school bus provided a ride to school. He had on a black full-length bear skin coat. He was one of a kind. He had black hair and black eyes and a black goatee, at a time in the south when that kind of stood out. I liked him from the start. Even though he was from a good family, and we went to the same church, I was not allowed to go out with him unless Tami or Joyce went with me. So, most of the time it was Jo. Far less complaints! His name was Darrell Reeves.

Going out consisted of riding around (cruising) a circuit, Hamburger hut, Tastee Freeze, Court square, Daniel Boone Drive and up to Oasis and back again! This could go on all night! Maybe you stopped and got a bite to eat, maybe just a cherry coke. It depended on how much money your date had. Darrell always had plenty! His Dad was a mason and he was his gopher! He hated it, but it paid well and he always said someday he would be CEO and someone would be his gopher! Sure, enough he did!

Darrell loved Tom T. Hall and I can still remember me and Darrell and Joyce riding down the river in Bob's old green Silverado truck with Tom singing. Darrell was my first beau and will probably be my last. He was married four times. He was excellent in business, not so good at marriage. Between marriages he would call me and we would get together as old friends, nothing more. But I loved him and when he died he left a hole as big as Texas in my heart, but as they say if you remember they are never gone. So today as I sit crying listening to ole Tom, here's to you Darrell.

Chapter 27
Learning to Crochet

My Maw taught me many wondrous things! I wish I could remember half of them. I wish I had listened more and talked less, a hard thing for me! Down the road from where I grew up there was an old General Store. James Hawn and his wife Abby ran it. It had all kinds of things beside food staples. There were boots and shoes and some Sunday dresses. My first 'real' jeans came from there. Turtle Backs with huge bell bottoms! I loved them and wore them forever! There were little dollar toys, like pads that you could write on with a little plastic pen. Then you raised the plastic and it erased it and you could do it all over again, but what I wanted most was a little knitting and crocheting set.

    My Mother didn't know how to crochet but my Maw did! I begged and pleaded until Mom bought me the little set. I couldn't wait to get to Maw's the next weekend for my lesson. Maw made doilies; fancy ones that were shaped sometimes like Roosters, or would have giant starched stiff flowers which adorned the "front" room tables. I wanted to make one of those! We set down on the porch swing with her "big" hands wrapped around the thin cotton twine. They moved fast and deftly as she made a row of chain stitch. She reminded me to count the stitches as it was important to the outcome. I was mesmerized! My fingers and hands were clumsy, and the thread got caught and knotted and I had to start again, but she was oh so patient. I can see her now peering down over her glasses, deep in trying to teach me how to do this task! Each time I faltered she carefully placed my hands back where they were supposed to be and we would start again. After a while my movements became almost as fluid as hers. I was elated! I didn't make many doilies but later on I found just the right project for my talent. When I became pregnant with my son Brent!

    I was living in Norwood, Ohio and Don worked four until two am. I thought a baby afghan would just be perfect and proceeded to acquire the yarn I needed. Yellow would be just right, since we didn't know the gender. Not like now! I thought a ripple would be beautiful so I began. I crocheted and crocheted and Don kept buying me yarn. Once he said he thought it might be a little big for a crib, but I kept crocheting. Until finally it became apparent that this was a bedspread and not a crib blanket! I had forgotten the golden rule of crocheting: count your stitches! Since I was using yarn not twine, it was a monster! It was so heavy you could barely lay under it and move. I kept it for years. It went with me everywhere I moved! It was a memory of a happy time and my Maw's tutelage! I wish I could remember how to do it now.

Chapter 28
The Uniform

Fall is in the air and Football season is here! It always reminds me of Band practice and Majorette Drills. Deborah Jarvis Evans and I were best friends and majorettes together. Probably a bad combination. We were partners in crime. I loved her and still do. She had this huge mane of dark hair. It was curly and she was continually trying to straighten it. I on the other hand had no hair at all! On Friday's while the other girls were spending hours at the beauty shop getting their hair done in huge pompadour ringlets so the tiaras could be shown to their best I sent my hair in a box to Kathy Garland by Mom. It cost $5.98 at KMART. I kept two just in case something happened to one. It was a frosted wiglet. Absolute match to my wispy hair.

    We, Deb and me, were the bane of the other girls. We were different. Once we decided our boots (white cowboy with huge tassels) didn't make enough noise. So, we took them and had heavy cleats put on toes and heels and surprised them all during the Daniel Boone Festival Parade. Together we sounded like a herd of horses. SURPRISE!

All school year we had sales to raise money for new majorette uniforms! New sexy ones! White sequin ones with halter backs! At pep rallies and at every event imaginable we sold chips, pop, candy, gum,etc.

Well, let me explain! I have always wondered; well maybe thought I was picked for majorette for what I could bring to the table, literally. I was in a lot of things now that I think about it. Maybe for the same reason. The Yearbook staff, the choir, drama club, and others. All of which were charitable organizations. To be more precise my step father owned a potato chip company and sold snack foods. AH HA! Does it make sense now? Well after many bake sales and pep rallies we made up enough to buy our little sexy outfits! They sure turned heads! We felt like the ROCKETTES. At Christmas of my senior year I graduated and went on to college. Leaving high school and the Majorettes behind!

A few weeks ago, I was having lunch with my old BFF, I was reminded that Knox Central

refused to give us our diplomas until we returned our Majorette uniforms.
 "Did you get your diploma?" she asked.
"Yes."
"Did you send your uniform back?" she said.
 "I must have", I said. "Did you?"
 "No!"
I wonder where my uniform is? Wish I had kept it!

Chapter 29
Traveler's Inn

The other day there was a post on Facebook showing a picture of the old Traveler's Inn Motel and Restaurant. It is gone now, but it sure held some memories for me. Some that definitely changed the course of my life.

In the spring of 1974 I was living the life of a college freshman. I was newly emancipated to the dorm life of Cumberland College. The summer before I had met and started dating a man, five years older than me. He was tall, dark, and handsome with the striking good looks of Cat Stevens. He had a brooding way about him. He didn't say much. Years later I found out why, he had nothing to say. I could look over that; passion and lust superseded intelligence. I could live with that.

When my Mother met him, all bets were off! It wasn't going to happen! Donald Gray was a MAN! Not one of these little boys I had been seeing. It was war! For my graduation at Christmas she bought me a new car; a bribe! It was to make sure Mr. Gray would move on down the line.

I found college life liberating. No more Mom looking over my shoulder, no more Don checking up on me either. After a while I began having new young college suitors and Don soon took notice and pressured me to get married.

One Sunday evening after spring break and on my way back to school Don wanted to go for a ride and talk about it. We weren't alone, his cousin Harold Mills and his girlfriend were with us. As would have it, I parked my new car in the parking lot of Travelers Inn. Big, big mistake!   We drove around awhile and just talked. In the meantime, Leonard Mills, who owned the service station where my step dad serviced his chip trucks, was having dinner at the restaurant and spied my car. As any good Samaritan would do, he proceeded to call my Mother and ask why it was parked at the Travelers Inn Motel. Need I say more?

Well let me describe my Mother. The women of my family are direct descendants of Cherokee Indians. We do not trail off like limbs from a trunk we have our own. They are like lions protecting their cubs, they will fight to the death even if it kills the cub.

Upon returning to the car I found my Mother going thru every room of the motel looking for me. There were men and women some married, some not, some to each other, some not, some clothed, some not, looking in amazement at this crazed woman with this German Rugger gun! She had my Dad's gun!

She saw us and she proceeded to use it! I can still see Donnie now. He started to run. He is six feet three inches tall and at that time skinny as a rail. She shot at his feet first and both feet jumped high. I never saw a man run so fast. He ran to Wilbur Bingham's Chevron and got in the Telephone booth with bullets whizzing all around. I think the Rugger must've held nine bullets but it jammed and by now Chester had wrestled it away from her. If he hadn't there probably wouldn't have been a Donald Brent! Well you can guess what happened next! eighteen years old and the last whipping I ever got. The next Friday Don and I eloped! Talking about cutting your nose off to spite your face.

Chapter 30
Laughter

My Maw taught me many things. One of them is the joy of laughter! I can still see her now, laughing until she cried at some ole joke that family would tell her. She had a bawdy sense of humor and loved little "dirty" jokes. Not "dirty" like now, but farmer's daughter jokes! She would cringe at TV and the language no.! She had a big laugh. One that made her shake all over and take her glasses off to wipe a stray tear! I loved to make her laugh.

   Sometimes now I find myself laughing at things she did or said, and I feel closer to her than ever. Yesterday I was sharing an event about her with my good friend and we both laughed until we were crying, too. She had a habit of visiting unannounced and at a very early hour! Usually around seven thirty or eight am. One such visit occurred shortly after Don and I were married. She showed up to investigate my housekeeping. She never knocked and always just yelled to tell you she was there. Her first critique was the bathroom where she could also checkout the bedrooms on the way; making sure they were made up and tidy.

This morning Don and I were having a little "alone" time when we heard the door open and Maw call out my name! My heart jumped into my throat as I knew she would start looking for me if I didn't answer soon. I yelled back I would be there in just a minute. I could hear her opening and shutting doors. I whispered to Don to hurry get dressed or we would be caught! I reached for whatever I could to put on. By now I was in full panic mode! I finally made it out just before she made her entrance and made a quick excuse about being slow to greet her.

She looked at me over her glasses and said, "You aren't still in bed at this time of day? Are you?" She looked me over from head to toe, stopping at my drawers! I had put on Don's underwear instead of my shorts! "Well, Deb is this some new fashion?" she said. I cringed! She stayed no longer than thirty minutes. She never did. Don stayed hid while she was there. I don't know if it was because I had his underwear or he dreaded to face Maw!

Maw went next door to visit Mom, and she must've told her about the visit because later my mother laughed and laughed at Maw's recollection of it! Apparently, my Maw knew everything and me, wearing Don's shorts, gave it away! She "visited" all of the family just the same! No knocking just walking right on in! What I would give for one of those visits now.

***

The telephone has sure come a long way since I was growing up! Everyone has one. Even six-year old's have one. Yesterday Joyce Logan and I went shopping and out to lunch. The child sitting next to us, maybe six years old, was texting someone. Who knows who? His stock brokers?

When I was growing up you had one phone! A big black rotary one, for those of you with touch pads it means you dialed it, that weighed approximately twenty pounds. It was located in the "front room" where everyone one could hear your conversation! Most of us had "party" lines. In other words, you had a specific ring. It may have been one long, or one long and one short or two long, etc. It worked pretty well for rural areas with few telephone lines.

For years we were one of the few homes with a telephone and people would come from all around to use it, or if someone had bad news they would usually call our house to send it. Where now we have social media, back then we had social party lines! Little old ladies would listen in on conversations of neighbors to get gossip and news of the day! Well, "down the river" there were a few of them such ladies, but there was a gentleman, too! God rest his soul. John "dad" Bryant was the sweetest man you would've and could've ever met, but he had a vice. He loved to listen to Mae Lee, Ruby Evans, and Mae Bennett on the phone! John Dad was Chester's Dad. He was elderly and tended to all of us. He didn't drive and never ever raised his voice. He was a widower and he lived to take care of us. He would have just died if he had known we knew he overheard their conversations, mostly about recipes and who said what to whom!

 He would pick the phone up ever so gingerly and listen, and sometimes I would slip so silently in, and his shoulders would be shaking with silent laughter, his eyes crinkling at some funny story between two old ladies and I would tap him, mean I know, and he would quickly put it back on the hook. "I was checking to see if Chee could call", he would say! Calling Chester, Chee. I loved John Dad, as if he was my own, and when he died, I cried like a baby.

***

My butt has fell off! Well not literally, more like figuratively! Last week having lunch with an old BFF, as always, the topic of age arose! Did we look our age? Did we feel our age? Who was aging gracefully? We decided we didn't look too bad, considering what it took until now to look this good! We agreed Spanx helped, but getting out of the shower was quite depressing. She said the sagging skin on her arms and legs. I had a worse horror story to tell.

Upon exiting the tub and standing with my behind to a full-length mirror retrieving a towel from the floor I discovered to my horror, I had no buttocks! They were pancakes that had flattened and were sliding lower and lower and I would soon be folding them up and tucking them in my shoes! ARGH! I was shocked when it happened! I knew my pants were a little looser but I never knew my bottom had got up and left!

I then knew what my grandmother Rose meant years ago when I asked her how it felt to be old, she was probably sixty then. She looked very solemnly and said," I look in the mirror sometimes and say, "Who is that old woman

looking back at me!"
Maw, I know what you mean.

Chapter 31
My Babies

Tonight, as I was giving my babies a bath, my four-legged babies, the smell of the shampoo brought back memories of another day, another time. Smells do that to me! When I walk down the toiletries aisle and smell the Old Spice it reminds me of Larry Logan, a boy I went to grade school with. We traded names at Christmas and someone bought him soap on a rope. Old Spice soap on a rope. I think he washed his hair in it!

    Getting back to the dog shampoo, as a child I spent a lot of time with my maternal grandmother Rose Wilson. She was what you might say now a woman of character. She was a woman of independent means. She worked for the suffrage movement and the UMWA. She tended the farm while my grandfather worked for the mining company. She was what you would call a real go getter. She had eleven grandchildren and on any given weekend at least half would be at their old sprawling farm house, rooms tacked onto porches and when I was small an outhouse back behind the smoke house.

It was an adventure to ride the school bus over to their house carrying my church clothes and a pair of underwear in an old brown paper sack. For her it was two days of cheap labor! On one such weekend I returned home smelling quite odoriferous! My mother quite concerned asked," Deb, what have you done to your hair?" (Well those of you who know me know I have never had much hair!)

"Maw said this would make my hair grow thick and pretty and long."
"What did MAW have you do this weekend?", she said.
"Me and Den cleaned out the chicken house!" I said.
"Did she wash Den's hair with this miracle shampoo too!" Mom said.
"Oh yes!"

It wasn't until years later that I discovered we had been deloused.

***

Well as most of you know by now my Rollie Boy has went to his forever home. It was a hard decision for me to let him go. The two boys were the last to leave and had bonded not only to each other but to me as well. The family that adopted him had lost their fur child a week ago and were grieving. Their boxer was thirteen when he passed. I could tell by talking to them that Rollie would be loved and cared for as no other. What more could anyone hope for?

    My thoughts returned to nearly two years ago when I lost my Sami. Even now I can barely speak his name. For fourteen years he was my constant companion. He was there after I lost my mother and when Brent went away to law school. No one can ever know how much he meant to me. He kept me from being swallowed up into the darkness of depression when my diabetes became unbearable! He gave me the incentive to pull myself up to care for him when I could not care for myself. There were days when I had no one to speak to but him. His love was sent to me from Heaven.

    So, when these people said they had a hole in their home. I knew they had a hole in their heart too. I hope tonight way over in Virginia a little brown puppy has made three people a little happier and a little less sad!

***

Rockie had his vet visit yesterday. He is getting

quite good at going! It seems we are going every week. With all the shots, the sprain, the diarrhea and now more shots due in two weeks, he is learning the personnel quite well. He is also learning to be a good traveler. From my house to Dr. Mike's is almost fifty miles and highway 92 is a curvy road!

When we got there the office and yard was packed! That's what I get for waiting until Saturday, I thought. After checking in we sat down to wait! There were various breeds in house and Rockie was enthralled. His little tailless butt wiggled each and every time some new critter arrived. There was an Alaskan malamute, a white Westie, a Weimaraner, and other beautiful animals, but then a Lady arrived with a non-descript carrier. It was quiet and not a whine could be heard. She sat down a couple seats over and we began to exchange niceties. All this time Rockie was snooping ever so gently around the back and sides of the carrier. He sniffed and he sniffed until he got to the front. About the time he did, this black and white cat jumped and hissed and shook that crate as if it was going to break free and attack! Rockie squealed and took a flying leap landing square in my lap, shaking as if a pit bull had got him! His little mouth was shivering and he was whimpering and everyone in the place was laughing!

Rockie stayed in my lap for the rest of our visit. When Dr. Mike saw him, he was twenty-seven pounds at twelve weeks. He said he was going to be one big dog! I tend to think that the next time 'ole ROCK sees a cat I might should run!

Chapter 32
Girlfriends

As I grow older I am growing bolder! Yesterday a dear friend and I were having lunch at Red Lobster in Richmond. I love Red Lobster (unsolicited endorsement). We had heard that it was going to shut its doors, all of them, and we were in a panic thinking, "No more crab fest, lobster fest, shrimp fest, no more Bahama Mamas." How could they?! So, we made a day out of "pretend" shopping so we could eat and have an early cocktail in case the Facebook rumor was true!

    The lunch was fantastic! I would post a pic but it would just cause undue mayhem to all those of you who cannot get to Richmond, Lexington or Knoxville. I have never understood why they have to be one hundred miles away.

    After glutting ourselves the waiter asked very kindly would we want a dessert. Well after inducing 3500 calories orally a couple thousand more couldn't hurt. So, we kindly agreed upon the Chocolate Wave and this Strawberry Shortcake thing. It looked harmless enough. When it came, the Chocolate Wave was to my friend's delight stupendous! Mine on the other hand was not quite edible! Upon reflection I decided I must mention it to my server! My companion was not so sure. When he came to deliver our bill I kindly reiterated that the dessert was not fit to eat (in not so many words). He said he would call his manager and when he came he asked, politely, what was the problem.

    I asked did anyone ever complain about this strawberry thingy? He said everyone seems to like it! I said they just aren't telling you, it is not good! Not good at all! I am so sorry to tell you! He looked at me and I looked at him and we both started to laugh. He said let me give you a new dessert on the house! By now I knew I didn't need any and I declined. But I told him I appreciated it anyway. He was really nice! I left a big tip! Older! Bolder! No, I think I am channeling Rose Wilson, my grandmother!

***

    I am going blind!! Well not really blind, but maybe a little or, maybe, I was just a little preoccupied.

Today my friend Ida and I decided to take an adventure. It was a perfectly fine late summer day to put the top back on my VW and traipse about the countryside and end up where we may. We decided to go to Frakes and visit the nursery for flowers and to the junk store for "treasures". The nursery was closed, but I found treasures galore! I bought a beautiful lamp with a broken shade (no problem I can fix it) a bunch of panty hose (.50 cents, bargain) and a plate with dividers in it! Perfect! Excellent day! On the way back, we decided to go to Middlesboro to eat at Cracker Barrel. Why not?

After having breakfast, which I enjoyed immensely she went to pay and I went to the "little girl's room". Now let me explain to all you ladies out there. Never take it for granted that all Cracker Barrels ladies rooms are on the right! YEAH!!! I was in a hurry or I was blind or I was about to pee. Take your pick, but I was on the pot when I saw the shoes pass by under the stall. My heart skipped a beat! Why had I not noticed the urinals, you think to yourself. I have asked that too! I broke out in a sweat thinking, should I just wait it out or make a run for it! Some people would've done that. Not me, I made a run for it! A man was standing

with his back to me, thank God! Hopefully, I'll never see him again! I saw Ida and grabbed her by the back of her shirt and said, "Let's get out of here, quick!"
"What's wrong," she said.
"I've been where no woman's been before."

Chapter 33
Scotch

Everyone has embarrassing moments. I surely have had mine. One such episode happened not to me, but in my presence and left an indelible mark on my memory!

In probably 1987 or 1988 I was working at Manchester Hospital. I didn't get much time off then, but when I did I would plan little adventures, short but memorable. That fall Mikhail Baryshnikov, the famous dancer, was appearing in Knoxville. So, I made a plan to get the best seat I could afford and stay at the Hyatt next door and eat at the best place. For one night all bets were off. I bought a new dress and dyed my hair and I was off. Upon arriving I indeed discovered I had a great seat. It was down near the orchestra. Not directly, but pretty close. I got there early so I could peruse the pretty ladies in all their finery and the handsome men arriving in their black tuxes. For Knoxville this was a big event to get such a world-renowned persona to visit their quant little city! My seat was in the last row on the left side on the floor level. The center aisle was to my right with one seat between me and the aisle. There was a slight grade, in other words it went downhill! I hadn't been sitting there too long when too my amazement Johnny Majors, football coach of Tennessee, sat down in the empty seat to my right. He had in his left hand what appeared to be a beverage of an intoxicating nature. The odor of it believed it to be scotch. He seemed to be enjoying himself heartily! People paraded in until it was nearly full. Knoxville being as it is mostly a small southern city and mostly everyone who is anyone knowing everyone else, they were chatting and mingling amongst their selves. I was taking this all in! Along about the time the orchestra was starting these two couples began making an entrance. You could tell they must have been somebody! They were dressed to the nines. Men in their tuxes, the ladies had their furs. This one lady was really dressed. She was out front and her dress was red I'll never forget it! About half way down the aisle she got her heels hung up in her skirt and she started tumbling. She not only fell she rolled! Head over butt. All the way down to the front. People were standing, concerned! But Johnny Majors half lit started laughing, and laugh he did! I thought I would die. The woman was horrified and skulked back to her seat trying to act nonchalant, as if nothing out of the ordinary had happened. I can still see that poor woman with her fancy hair all over her head and her butt up in the air and Johnny Majors cackling like a crow!

Chapter 34
Bus Monitor

This morning was my second day of school (I'm not a student). I am a bud monitor! Yes, the low man on the totem pole; The lowest of the low! But I get to see the clean, fresh, smiling faces first thing in the morning. When they are young and looking forward to the new day.

You remember those times. When you have the new backpack and shiny sparkling shoes! I do! When my hair was slick and smelled good and I had a fresh pad of note paper that didn't have anything written on it!

This year I have a new driver. He is different. He has tattoos on his arms, wears overalls and doesn't say a whole lot (to me that is). But the children love him. They are small, our children, and different too. In all kinds of ways. They call him Leslie Dale. His whole name. It's kind of sweet. He knows each and every one. He has had them since they started school, he said! When they get on the bus he greets each with a smile and a pleasantry, they in turn reciprocate. The trip seems uneventful to those who do not know what could have been, but in those short moments a bond occurred between driver and student. My year is just starting I feel I am in very capable hands. I am sure the parents of these students feel the same!

***

This morning I watched an 8-year-old do something that caused me to quake inside with uncontrolled laughter! She never saw me, and I never let on, but it was all I could do to hold it in!

    I am a bus monitor and she sat directly across from me on the front row. As she sat down she proceeded to rummage around in her "Hello Kitty" back pack for an important item. She brought out what looked to be some "pricey" pieces of makeup and proceeded to apply them with a ham-handed result. One could tell she was not quite adept. She applied the blush first, and as she had no mirror, no concept of the amount. Next the crème foundation, thus smearing blush. By this time, I was more and more fascinated. Out of the corner of my eye I watched her apply the glittery eye shadow, mascara, and then the lipstick. I could tell by the time we entered the school, the way she walked she really thought she had a handle on this and she looked good. I never said a word. I didn't want to burst her bubble, but I remembered a time when I was young.

In 1963 I was seven years old and in second grade. I was in Grace Bennett's class and it was picture day. My mother was so excited for me. We had rolled my hair the night before in pink sponge rollers. And I wore my red corduroy jumper with the white shirt trimmed in red. Before leaving for school that day I decided I needed a little something extra. I had just lost my two front teeth and was feeling a little self-conscious. I had a plan. My Mother was always so beautiful and put together. She wore makeup. So, I would slip and put some in my little black patent leather pocketbook for later that morning.

I slipped and got Mom's powder, eyebrow pencil, and her ravishing red lipstick. And while I was at it I got her bluebird earrings, just for that added touch. I held my pocket book so tight all the way to school, so afraid someone might get wind of what I was going to do.

First thing off the bus, I went straight to the

girl's bathroom to apply my face. I powdered my nose (just like Mom). I drew on my eyebrows, and carefully did my lips in ravishing red. Then the topping on the cake, Mom's blue bird earrings.

I walked straight to the gym and got in line with my class to get their picture made. I saw a few looks, but I assumed it was because of how gorgeous I looked. Mrs. Bennett was way up front with all the other teachers not really paying any attention to me. I got my picture made and when I was seen, I was promptly taken to the restroom and washed thoroughly. I assumed grumpy Mrs. Bennett just had a thing against makeup until my mother got my school pictures. I was so excited! I thought I looked beautiful. I jumped off the bus and ran thru the door and shoved them to her with my big smile.

Thru the plastic sleeve, looking back, was a seven-year-old, tousled headed girl with a big toothless, ravishing red grin and crooked black eyebrows, framed with two big bluebird rhinestone earrings! I saw the color drain from her face. We didn't buy those pictures! I wish we had!

RAVISHING RED VELVET CAKE
2 1/2 cup all-purpose flour

1 tsp baking soda
1 tsp cocoa
1 1/2 cups sugar
2 eggs
1 1/2 cups canola oil
1 tsp vinegar
1-ounce bottle red food coloring
1 tsp vanilla
1 cup buttermilk

FOR THE CREAM CHEESE ICING
1/2 cup margarine
1 8oz package cream cheese
1 box confectioners' sugar sifted
1/2 tsp vanilla
1 cup chopped lightly toasted pecans
FOR THE CAKE; Preheat oven to 350 degrees. Grease and flour 3, 9-inch round cake pans. Sift flour, baking soda and cocoa together. Beat sugar and eggs in large bowl. In a separate bowl
mix oil, vinegar, food coloring and vanilla. Add the eggs and sugar and beat until combined. Add
the dry ingredients alternating with the buttermilk ending with the dry ingredients. Pour into pans, tapping to release bubbles. Bake for 25 minutes. Cool for 10 minutes

before frosting.
FOR THE CREAM CHEESE FROSTING; Let all ingredients come to room temp. Cream well. Add vanilla and nuts. Spread between layers and on tops and sides and chill.

Chapter 35
The Day My World Stopped

There are very few days in our lives that are indelibly etched in our memories. I am assured of one, October 3, 1970.

My father had been sick for the better part of six years. The long and arduous trek to the V.A. Hospital in Louisville had played havoc on our little family. My Maw had cared for me and my sister for long spans of time as my mother had stayed in Louisville with him. The five-hour trip was just too long and expensive to make too often and until April 1970 the V.A. didn't recognize his illness as service connected. No disability benefits, so she stayed with friends and family and we stayed with Maw.

The Friday before that day, we had made arrangements to take the whole family to Louisville to visit Daddy. He was to have a pace maker inserted Monday. He told mom not to come until he called, it turned out to be prophetic. The next morning at around five-thirty my mother woke me, she was worried. "I just know something is wrong!" she said, as she drank her strong black coffee I still can see her, the phone rang. The color left her beautiful face as I could hear a voice say:" Mrs. Davis I'm sorry to tell you, Mr. Davis has passed away." Yes, no, yes, was all she could say. My stomach wretched and I became ill. I never knew I could actually feel that sick all over my body.

At around five that morning the orderly came by the ward where my daddy was. He was awake, he spoke to the orderly as they passed the ice and water. At around five-thirty, just about the time when my mother woke me, the nurse arrived to pass his medicine. He had gone, just like that. Closed his eyes and left this earth, thirty-eight years old, father of two, husband of the love of his life, gone! I always believed he knew that he might not be there that Saturday, because we were going to leave at four am to get there by nine or ten am to eat breakfast with him. Somehow, I think he knew.

In the days that ensued, I was in a fog and to this day there are only bits and pieces that remain, but that morning I remember it all as if it was yesterday. That feeling of illness and unbelief and how my mother looked. She was never the same, none of us were. My sister went into a type of catatonia that remained for years. I was, for all intents and purposes, the head of the household after that. My mother somehow never regained her strength of who she once was.

As we sat under that tent on that bright October day and the shots rang out over Golden's Creek, the navy seaman handed my mother the trifold flag, and her shoulders shook in her black dress. She didn't utter one sound, she just shook. I didn't move, I wanted to scream, but I knew Daddy would have none of it. I was better than that, he raised me to be stronger than that. I would not cry, not right now. Not in front of these people. My sister didn't either, she sat quietly never moving, stoically. Her eyes straight ahead. It was if she was somewhere else. I look back and wonder how I coped, and then I knew, My Maw. She had given me the mechanisms I needed to become what I needed then, as well as now.

In the years that would follow, I would face illness, cancer, diabetes, divorce, single parenthood, losing my mother, bankruptcy and an illness of my son. But because of her strength and what she imparted to me, I am a survivor, an overcomer and as I look in the mirror I see bits and pieces of her looking back at me. Thank you, Maw! If I never told you, I love you.

The stories in this book span for fifty-eight years. Most of the people have died, but all have left lasting memories in my life. Some happy, some sad, some joyous, but mostly they are all love. Without them I am not who I was or who I have become.

www.ingramcontent.com/pod-product-compliance
Lightning Source LLC
Chambersburg PA
CBHW032043290426
44110CB00012B/926